Mel Bay Presents

Country Ballads & Waltzes for the Guitar

by Larry McCabe

A stereo cassette tape of the music in this book is now available. The publisher strongly recommends the use of this cassette tape along with the text to insure accuracy of interpretation and ease in learning.

Table Of Contents

Songs

Introduction

This book contains many new waltzes and ballads for pick-style acoustic guitar. The music notation is supplemented with tablature. Note reading, while desirable, is not required.

The country waltz is a mainstay of folk festivals and anywhere else country music is performed. This collection will help to satisfy the current shortage of new waltzes for the guitarist.

In popular music the ballad is generally regarded as a pretty or sentimental tune. In folk music, the terminology "ballad" is not restricted to the sentimental piece. For example, many folk ballads (Jesse James; Davy Crockett; Jed Clampett) are actually very upbeat tunes, suitable for adaptation to solo acoustic guitar.

Each song is presented in three forms. First, there is a basic melody. Following this is a basic guitar arrangement of the melody ("version one"). Finally, a more developed or challenging arrangement ("version two") is provided. Novice players can enjoy their progress from the basic to the more advanced material. Intermediate players will find interest in studying the arranging concepts used to develop each tune.

For best results in interpretation (and for listening enjoyment) use the cassette tape available for this book. The songs are ordered alphabetically but may generally be played in any order (remembering that the first arrangement of each melody is the easiest). Have fun playing them.

How To Read Tablature

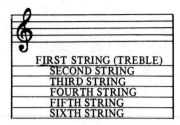

Tablature is a system designed to pinpoint the location of notes on the fingerboard. The tablature in this book appears directly underneath the music staff. Tablature consists of six lines, with the space above each line used in reference to a specific string.

If we wish to show the exact location of a note, we simply write the number of the fret it is found on in the appropriate (string) space. The open third string (G) is shown in the example at the left. Open strings are identified by the number "O".

When notes are "stacked" on top of one another like in the example at the left, play them all at once as you would a chord.

The example at the left shows a second fret on the fourth string.

Standard notation time values are paired with their tablature counterparts in the following illustration:

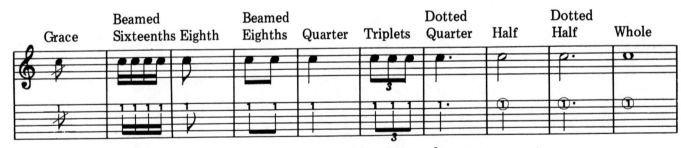

Fingerings

Where necessary, small numbers are attached to notes in the standard notation to indicate proper fretting-hand fingering.

The fretting-hand fingers are numbered as follows:
1 = Index Finger   2 = Middle Finger   3 = Ring Finger
4 = Little Finger   0 = Open string.

Symbols And Special Techniques

Slide-up Symbol /

"Sliding-up" is accomplished by the following:
1. Pick a fretted note. . . then,
2. "Slide" or move the fretting finger up the neck (without releasing finger pressure) to the next note.

The example at the left shows us to fret the D note on the second string, pick the string, then slide the first finger up from the third fret to the E note on the fifth fret.

Slide-down. Symbol \

Sliding-down is the reverse of sliding-up. The example to the left shows us to pick the second string at the third fret (while fretting with the first finger) and then slide the first finger back to the first fret while keeping pressure on the string.

Double-string slide. Symbol ⫽

The double-string slide requires sliding on two strings at once. Pick both notes, then slide as directed by the notation.

The hammer. Symbol ⌒H or ⌣H

To execute a hammer follow this procedure:
1. Play one note with the pick . . . then,
2. "Slam" (hammer) the indicated fretting-hand finger down on the second note (to make it sound without being picked).

In the example at left the third string is played open, then the second finger of the fretting hand strikes (hammers) at the second fret to sound the A note.

Result: one pick motion, two separate notes,

IMPORTANT: Despite this example, the hammer does not always "originate" from an open string.

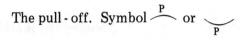

The pull-off. Symbol ⁀ or ‿

The pull-off is the opposite of the hammer. The example at the left shows us to:

1. Pick the second fret of the third string . . . then,
2. "Pull" the fretting finger from the second fret in such a manner to cause the second note (here, open G) to sound. Result: one pick motion, two separate notes.

The combination hammer/pull. Symbol ⁀ ⁀

This technique allows three separate notes to be sounded with one pick-motion. Execute as follows:

1. The first note is sounded with the pick.
2. The second note is sounded by hammering from the first note.
3. Without picking again, the third note is sounded by pulling off from the hammered note.

Each of the above examples represents a <u>slur</u> in which <u>one motion of the pick</u> (followed by a specific fretting-hand technique) <u>produces two (or more) different pitches in succession.</u>

Double-stops on non-adjacent strings.

When two notes are sounded together on non-adjacent strings it is often desirable to pick the higher note with the middle fingernail of the picking hand (upstroke) while playing the lower note with the pick (downstroke). In some cases a small "m" is attached to the upper note. This technique is not restricted to non-adjacent strings and may also be used to sound double-stops on neighboring strings.

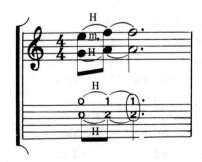

Double-hammer on non-adjacent strings.

The example at left should be played as follows:

1. Pick the open E with an up motion of the middle fingernail while picking the open G with a down motion of the pick.

2. Hammer from the open E to F with the first finger while simultaneously hammering from open G to A with the second finger.

Slur and pick companion string.

This technique is used many times in this book. It basically works like this:

1. Pick one note . . .
2. Slur to a second note (slide, hammer, or pull). . . . .
3. Pick a companion string (as indicated by the notation) at the moment the second note is sounded. See following examples.

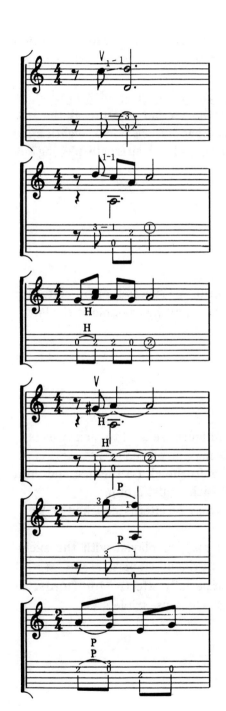

1. Pick the C note with an up-pick . . .
2. Slide the C to D on the second string
3. At the moment the D is sounded, pick the open fourth string D with a down pick.

1. Pick the D note with an up-pick . . .
2. Slide down to C. . .
3. Play open A (with a downpick) as C is sounded.

1. Play open G with a down-pick . . .
2. Hammer from open G to A . . .
3. Play C (up-pick) as A is sounded.

1. Play G sharp with an up-pick . . .
2. Hammer from G sharp to A on the third string. . .
3. Play open A (down-pick) as the A on the third string is sounded.

1. Play G with an up-pick . . .
2. Pull from G to F . . .
3. Play open A (down-pick) as the F note is sounded . . .

1. Play A with a down-pick . . .
2. Pull from A to open G . . .
3. Play D (up-pick) as the G note is sounded.

7

Basic Picking Technique

Symbols: ⊓ Down-Pick ∨ Up -Pick

Though no rules concerning picking technique are all-inclusive, the following information will help serve as a general guideline.

#1. Play down beats with a down-pick motion, as shown in the first measure at the left.

#2. Play up beats with an up-pick motion, as shown in the second measure at the left. Notice also that a succession of eighth notes should be played with alternate-picking motions.

#3. Alternate-pick a succession of sixteenth notes, as shown in the example at the left.

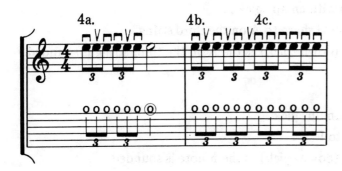

#4. Three techniques are used to pick triplets.

#4a. Triplets may be played (⊓∨⊓   ⊓∨⊓) with the downpick on the first and third note of each triplet group.

#4b. Triplets may be alternate picked (⊓∨⊓ ∨⊓∨).

#4c. Triplets may be played with the exclusive use of the down-pick (⊓⊓⊓   ⊓⊓⊓). This is especially effective for chord style rhythms which use triplets.

Chords

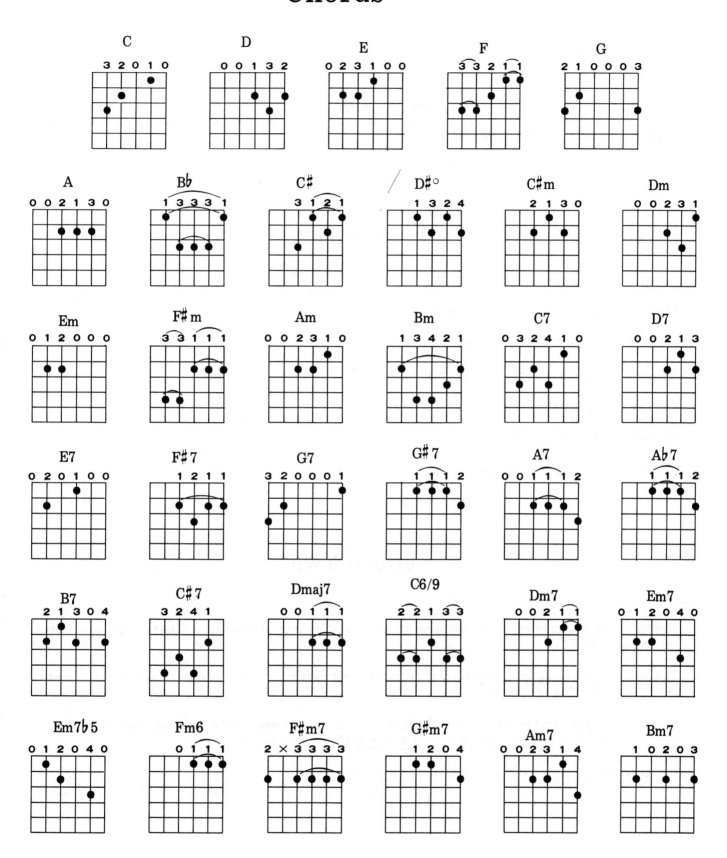

The above represent basic forms of the chords in this book. A variety of positions for each form may be found in <u>Mel Bay's Deluxe Encyclopedia of Guitar Chords</u> by Bill Bay.

Bakersfield Waltz

This waltz is played with a shuffle (♪♪ = ♪. ♪) rather than a straight eighth feel. It is set to a pretty chord progression and is not played too fast.

Version One

. Measures 1 - 8 are played mostly in first position.

. A half - barre is used for the F♯ minor chord in measure two.

. Measure 3 - 6 may be played in second position if the fourth finger is a problem.

. Measure 10 - 11 are played in the second position.

. In measure 12, shift back to the first position.

. The final two measures are played in the second position.

Version Two

. The index finger should cover the first three strings of the D chord in measure 1. The middle finger frets the second string.

. The slur and pick companion string technique is used in measures 1, 8 (first ending of part one) and measure 7 (second ending of part one).

. When repeating the first measure, "pinch" the interval on the first beat of the measure. Review the explanation for picking double stops on non-adjacent strings in the symbols section.

. A double-string slide is used in the next-to-last measure.

Bakersfield Waltz

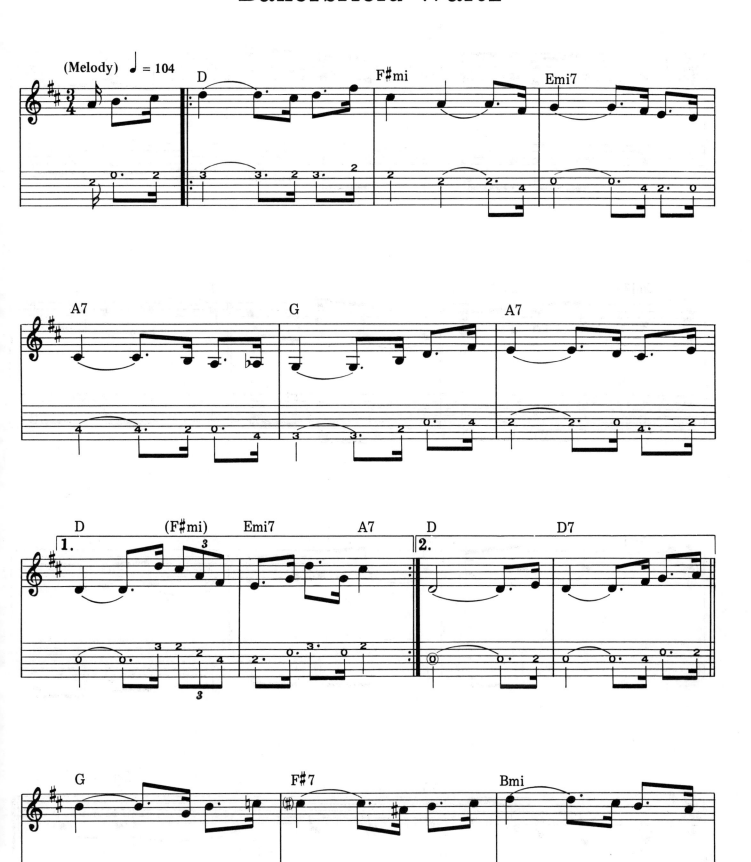

Bakersfield Waltz I

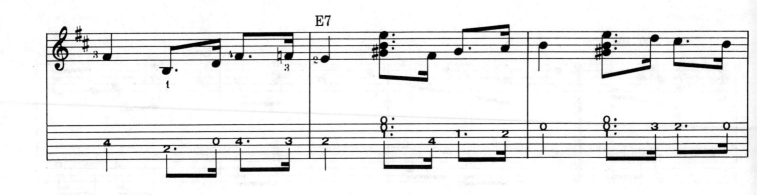

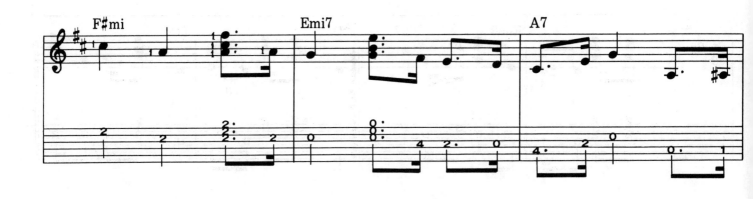

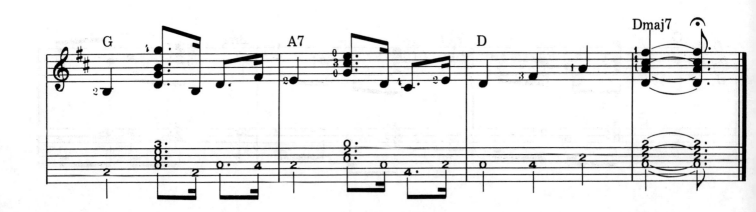

Bakersfield Waltz II

Balada de Mineros

This is a 6/8 ballad, same time signature as an Irish jig but played slower. "House of the Rising Sun" is a song often played in slow 6/8. The tune is in E minor but ends on an E major chord.

Version One

. This is a very simple arrangement. It is basically the melody with a chord added to the first beat of most measures.

. This arrangement is suggested for students needing practice with 6/8 time and basic chord fingerings.

Version Two

· This arrangement allows the student to use the fingers of the picking hand to pick out melody notes. It is suggested that the pick-if used at all-should be used only for bass notes played under melody notes.

. It is a good idea to study the bass and melody parts independently before attempting the solo.

. The combination hammer-pull technique is used in measures 1, 6, 9 and 14. It must be executed rapidly.

. The double-stops on non-adjacent strings technique is used throughout the solo. In such instances, the pick plays the lower note, if you are using a pick.

Balada de Mineros

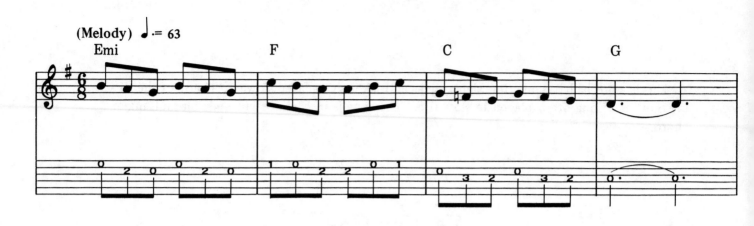

Balada de Mineros I

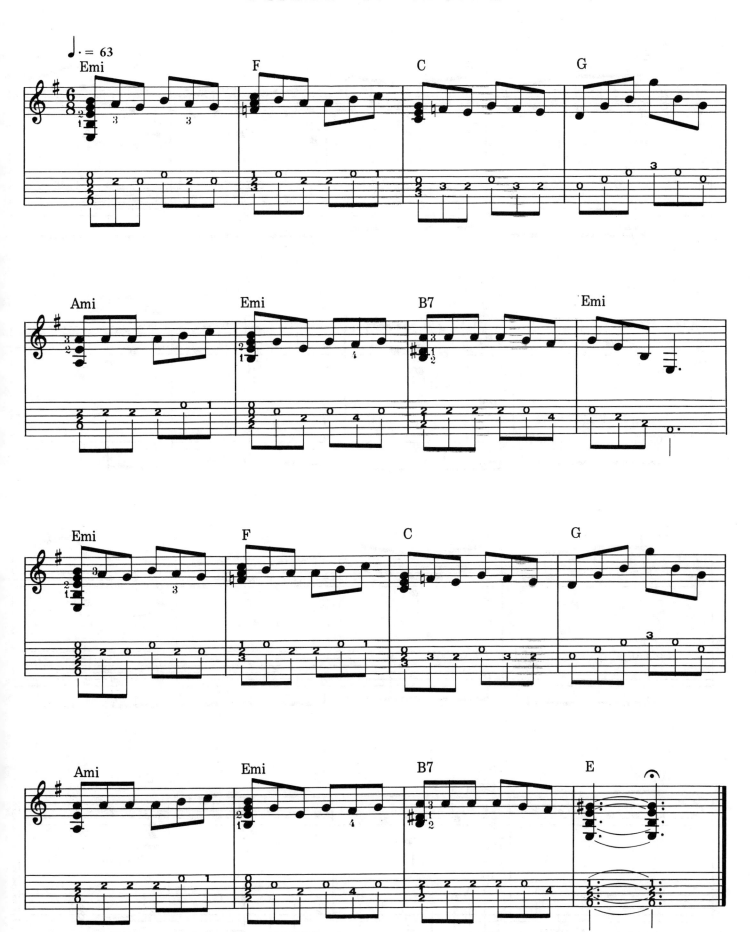

Balada de Mineros II

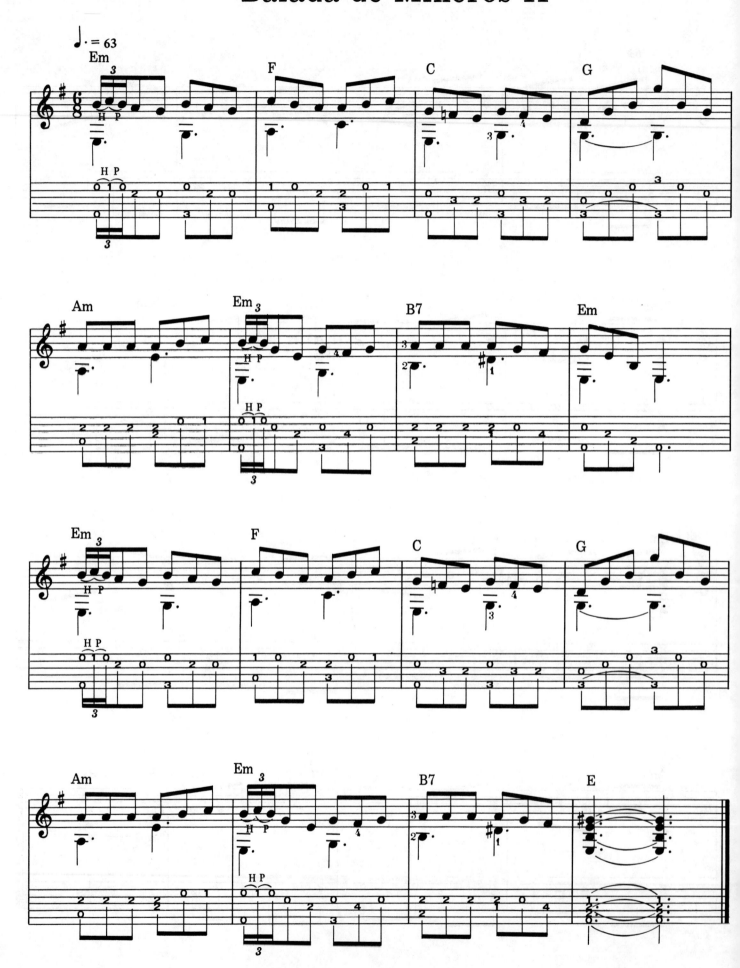

Black River Waltz

A simple country waltz using the basic rhythmic pattern (♩   ♩. ♪). The 32-bar length is quite commonly used for country waltzes.

Version One

. Play the chords lightly so the melody notes stand out. The hammers, pulls and slides should sound smooth and flowing and not rushed.

Version Two

. This arrangement incorporates the use of arpeggios in which the melody note is "surrounded" by chord tones (much like a banjo concept). In such cases it is best to bring out the melody note so that it stands out above the surrounding tones.

. The double-hammer on non-adjacent strings is used in measures 1, 9 and 17.

. The technique slur and pick companion string is used in various forms in measures 2, 8, 10 and 18.

. A double-string slide is used in measure 6.

. The ending of the song is rearranged for variety. The A♭7 measure (measure 32) requires the index finger to barre the fourth fret of the three bass strings while the ring finger plays the sixth fret (E♭) on the fifth string.

Black River Waltz

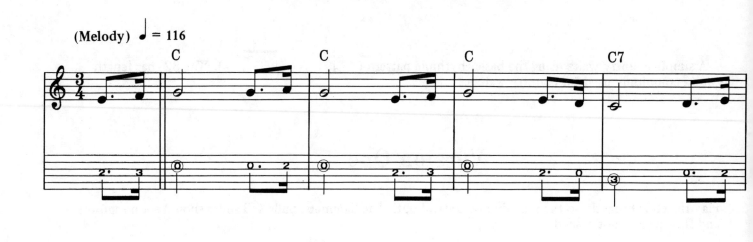

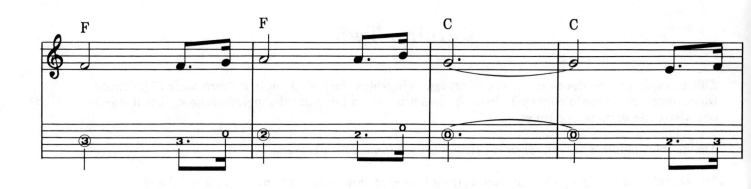

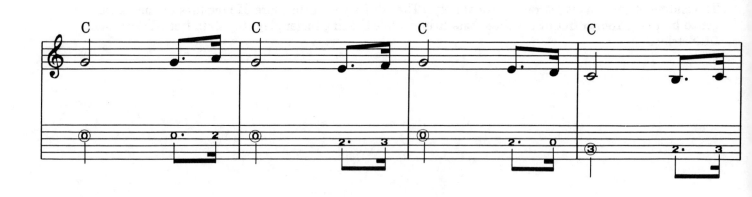

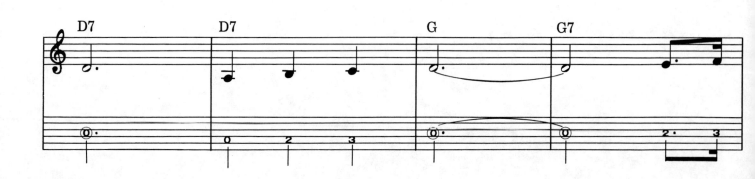

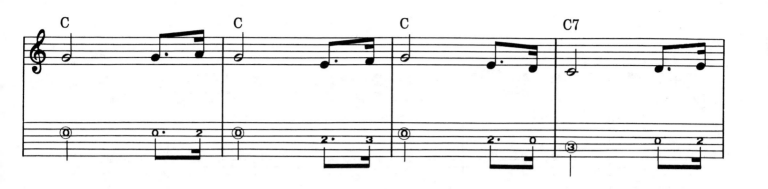

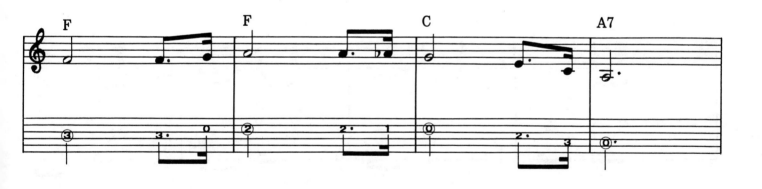

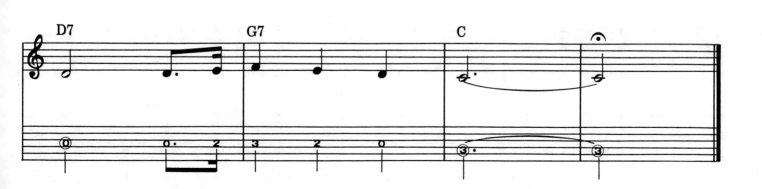

Black River Waltz I

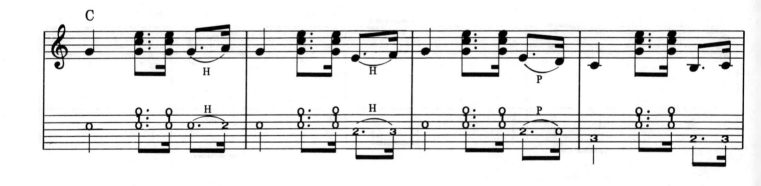

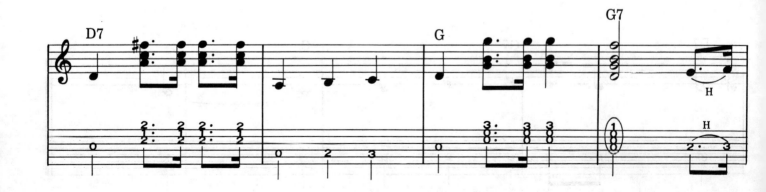

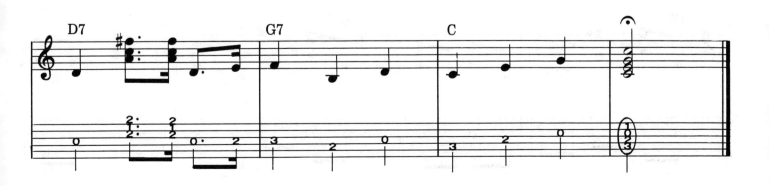

Black River Waltz II

Blue Snow

This is a slow sixteen - bar blues to be played with a triplet shuffle feel (♪♪ = ♩ ♪).

Version One

This simple adaption of the melody may be played in the first positon.

Blues make much use of the flatted third (G) and the flatted seventh (D)tones of the scale.

Be sure to use the fourth finger on the fourth frets and where otherwise indicated.

Version Two

. This arrangement uses a monotonic bass idea in several measures. This technique is common in the slow blues tunes.

. The slur and pick companion string technique is used in all but the final measure.

. Be sure to follow the fingerings closely for the smoothest result.

Blue Snow

Blue Snow I

Blue Snow II

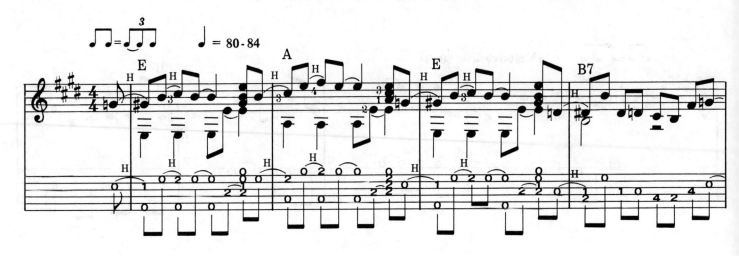

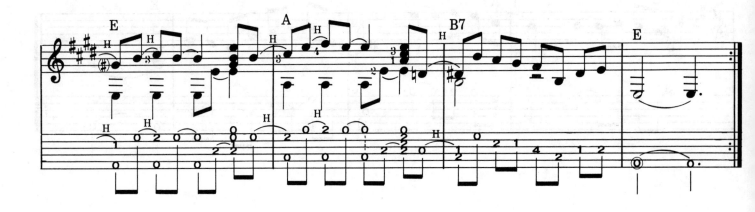

Boyd Walters' Favorite Waltz

A lively waltz to the rhythm ♩· ♫♫♫ using a compact 16 - bar structure.

Version One

. Basically this is the melody with eighth-note chords used to fill in behind the sustained notes. It may be good to use a very, very slight accent on the first beat of each bar. There are no slurs in this arrangement at all and it is imperative that the picking be down on the downbeats and up on the upbeats. Left-hand fingering is simple as the fourth finger is not used at all.

Version Two

. There isn't anything real fancy for technique here, but the song does roll along pretty good. The slur and pick companion string technique is used in measures one and nine. Try the hammers in these measures (1 and 9) <u>without</u> the "companion string" note (C) and you will appreciate how much it really does add to <u>use</u> this technique in your acoustic soloing.

. Be sure to use the fourth finger as indicated in the second, third, tenth and eleventh measures to keep the tune rolling smoothly.

Boyd Walters' Favorite Waltz

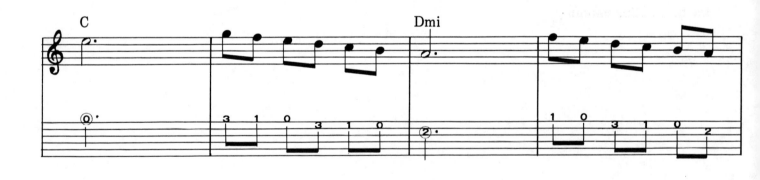

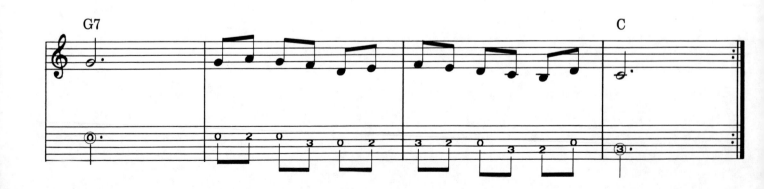

Boyd Walters' Favorite Waltz I

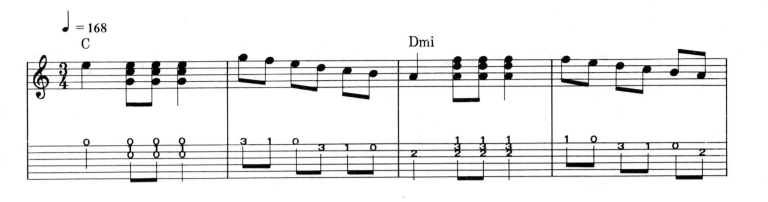

Boyd Walters' Favorite Waltz II

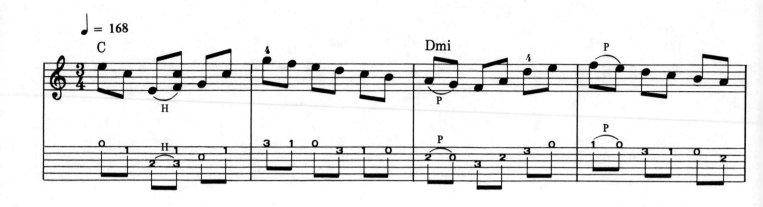

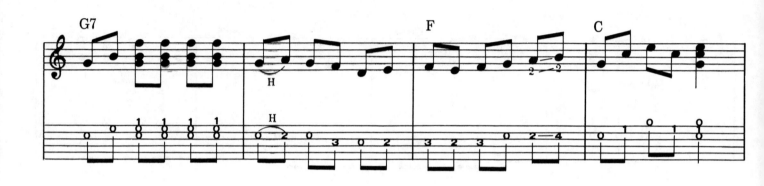

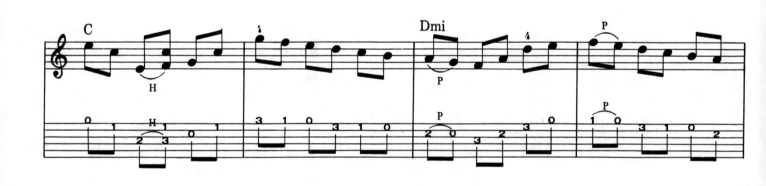

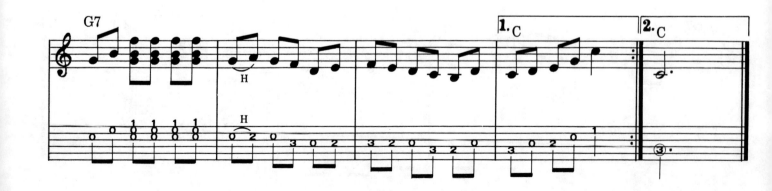

The Cricket Hunt

In folk music the term "ballad" is often applied to lively paced tunes concerning historical, nautical and folk hero, etc. subject matter. The Cricket Hunt is none of those, but it is lively and should be played with an open imagination.

The second section of the tune is played in relative (E) minor. Imagine the first half of the tune to the be hunt and the second half the capture.

Version One

. Like Black River Waltz I this tune is basically the melody filled with chord strums. The melody should of course be played slightly louder than the strums. I have known of players to prefer brushing the strums with a down-up motion of the middle fingernail. If this technique suits your style, feel free to use it.

Version Two

. This arrangement uses many grace-note hammers which propel the tune right along. The best sound will be produced by hammering fairly close to the fret.

. The melody is surrounded by rapid string-crossing arpeggios and alternate-picked chords. It is very essential to use alternate picking here. Acoustic guitar experts like Norman Blake and Doc Watson are masterminds of this tyle.

The Cricket Hunt

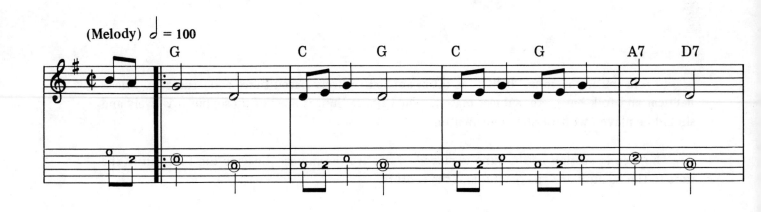

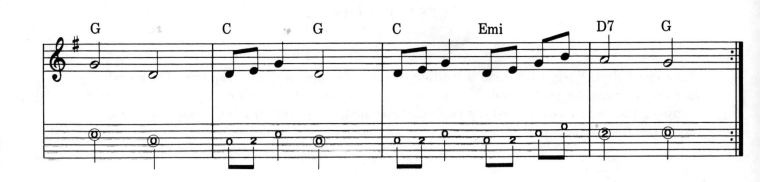

The Cricket Hunt I

The Cricket Hunt I

The Cricket Hunt I

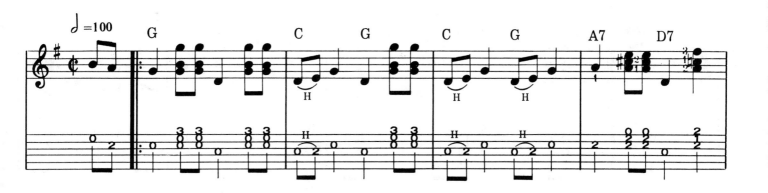

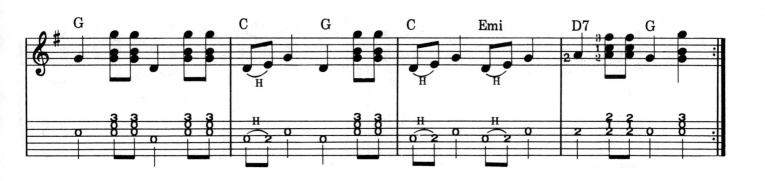

The Cricket Hunt II

Elizabeth's Waltz

This waltz may take a little extra practice to master.

Version One

. The first section of the tune (measures 1-8) requires use of the first and second positions. Follow the suggested fingerings closely and try to produce a smooth, ringing sound. There is a fairly good amount of fourth finger work in this section.

. The eighth notes in this piece are rather "lazy" and should not be played with a straight feel.

. In measure six roll the first finger from the D♯ to the G♯ to produce a smooth rather than choppy sound.

. In measure seven (the first measure of the first ending) be sure to plant the fingers so that the notes ring one after another and the open E sounds clearly.

. In the repeat of measure seven (the first measure of the second ending) again allow the notes to ring. Use a partial barre across three strings with the index finger. When adding the fourth finger try not to interfere with the sustain of the preceding notes.

. After sliding the ring finger to D♯ in the ninth measure leave it there to pick the D♯ again in the tenth measure.

. Be sure to finger measure fifteen as suggested. Allow the strings to ring by leaving the fingers down.

. The final eight measures are like the opening of the tune.

Version Two

. This is a fairly demanding piece which involves many unorthodox hand stretches. Throughout much of the piece it is desirable to leave the fingers in place on an arpeggiated chord form. This is so the notes can sustain and blend together clearly. A thorough study of the fingerings and symbols - combined with practice - can help achieve the desired sound.

. A half - barre across the first three strings is used in measures two and eleven.

. An "F - shape" A chord is used in the third measure. The first finger is lifted from the second string as open B is sounded.

. The double string slide is used in the fourth measure.

. Leave the fingers down through measures 6, 7, 8 etc. to achieve a full, ringing sound.

. The long stretch in the seventh measure will require extra practice.

. The slur and pick companion string technique is used in the seventh measure (for the first and second endings) of section one. It is also used in measures 8 (second ending of part one), 9, 10, 13, 17, and 18.

. A partial barre is used in measures ten and fourteen. Here, the first finger barres the second, third and fourth strings.

. A grand barre is used in the sixteenth measure (B7).

Elizabeth's Waltz

Elizabeth's Waltz I

Elizabeth's Waltz II

Foggy After Midnight

This song should be played with a trace of wistfulness.

Version One

. This is very basic and should present little problem.

. The chords in measures 1-8 and 13-17 are used to <u>fill space</u> between melody notes. They should not be played so loudly that they overpower the melody.

. The chords in measures 9-12 are used to <u>harmonize</u> under the actual melody notes. Leave the fingers in place on the chords and allow them to ring.

. Play the eighth notes with a swing feel.

Version Two

. This solo is almost entirely composed of double-stops with intervals of sixths. The middle finger should play the upper voice of each interval as the pick plays the lower voice. Of course, the lower note could be played by the thumb and the upper note by the index finger.

. This solo is not self-contained and needs accompaniment.

. A strong triplet rhythm is felt throughout the solo.

. The <u>double-string slide</u> is used in several places.

. The eighth-note rests in measures 9-12 can be accomplished by releasing pressure from the fretted notes while leaving the fingers in contact with the strings.

. In the twelfth measure, G is <u>hammered</u> to A while B simultaneously <u>slides</u> to C.

. An A minor is substituted for C in the final measure. To repeat the solo you might use a G major chord on the final two beats of the last measure to prepare for the return to the C chord.

Foggy After Midnight

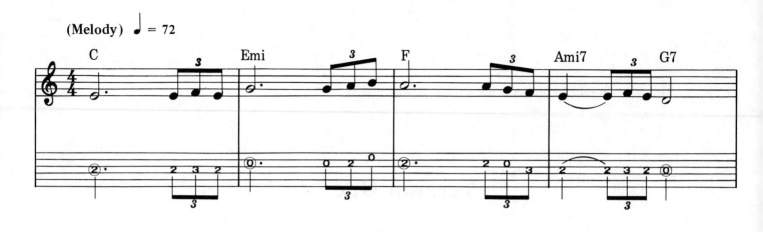

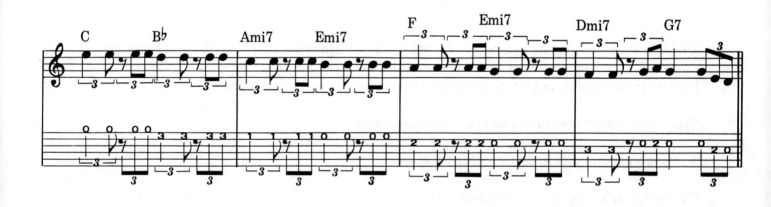

Foggy After Midnight I

Foggy After Midnight II

Halfstep Waltz

A fairly quick waltz with mixed rhythms. A glimpse at the chord progression reveals the meaning of the title.

Version One

. No slurs are used in this arrangement.

. Measures 2, 3, 5 and 6 may be played in either the first or the second position.

. Measures 10, 11, 14 and 18 may be played in the second position as indicated. Measure 19 should be played in the first position to prepare the hand for the B7 chord in measure 20.

. All of the above mentioned measures may be played in the first position as a good exercise for the little finger.

. This arrangement, like several others in this book, basically involves the strumming of simple chords used as fillers between melody notes. The recordings of the late Maybelle Carter best exemplify this style.

Version Two

. This is similar to version one except string-crossing arpeggios are often used here in banjo-like fashion to fill between notes. It is important that the melody be heard in these instances. Listening to the tape can be a great aid in interpretation.

. Be sure to use proper pick motion. Note the pick motion in measures 8 and 16.

. The above comments concerning measures 10, 11, 14 18 and 19 are applicable here.

. Note the use of the triplet in measures 10, 18 and 22.

Halfstep Waltz

Halfstep Waltz I

Halfstep Waltz II

Mellowtone Waltz

This one goes at a very leisurely pace with relaxed eighth notes. The chord progression is rather unusual and it may take a listening or two for your ear to adjust to it.

Version One

. Many chords are played between the melody notes and the fingerings must be watched closely. At times, fingers will be pressed down on single notes and kept there to be used in the chord which follows. See the first beat of the third measure (D note) for a good example of this.

. The melody should be brought out above the chords. As in many waltzes, a slight accent should be felt on the first beat of each measure.

. In the eighteenth measure, the first finger should slide from G♯ to A to get the hand in position for the following measure.

Version Two

. This arrangement often uses chords under the melody notes on the first beat of the measure (examples may be found in measures one and two).

. At other times an arpeggio will follow the melody note. An example of this is in measure three. Leave the second finger in place and allow the D note to ring as the B and F♯ are played.

. Another example of this idea is in measure four. Allow the open B to ring while following with the arpeggio. Once placed, leave the fingers down on the arpeggio to keep it ringing.

. The slur and pick companion string technique is used in measures 6, 8, 14, 22, 26-27, 29-30 and 31.

. There are several position shifts here and the fingerings should be studied closely for the smooth-est results. For example, in measure one the first finger slides from the second to fourth fret to prepare for the C♯ mi. chord which follows.

. Measures 16, 18 and part of 19 are played in the fourth position. Measure 17 is played in the third position. All of these measures offer a good opportunity to brush up on reading skills in the third and fourth positions.

. Measure 19 uses a B mi. chord in which the little finger must barre the seventh fret of the first three strings while the first finger plays the fourth fret of the fourth string. Note that in this measure we shift back to the second position to prepare for the following measure.

. When the same fret is played in succession on adjacent strings (as in measure 24), the finger should roll -- not jump -- from one note to the next.

Mellowtone Waltz

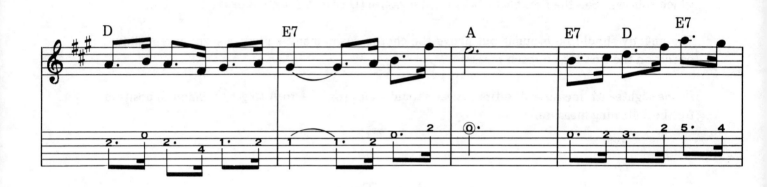

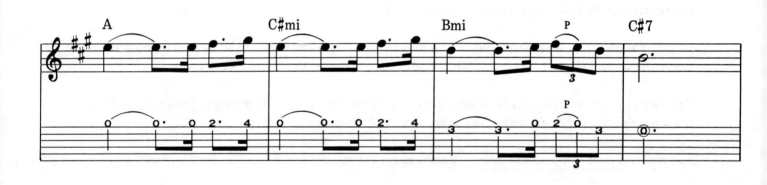

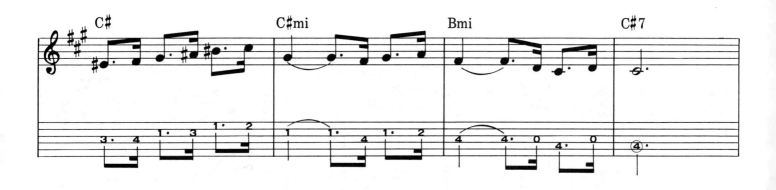

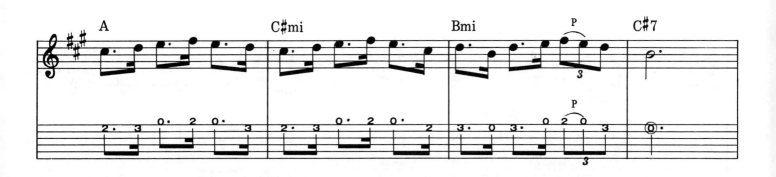

Mellowtone Waltz I

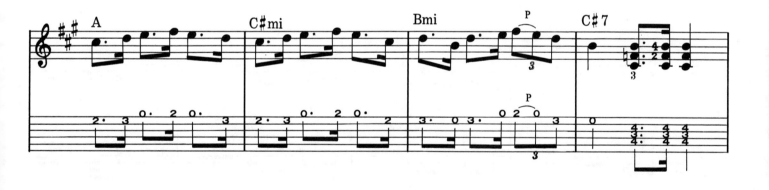

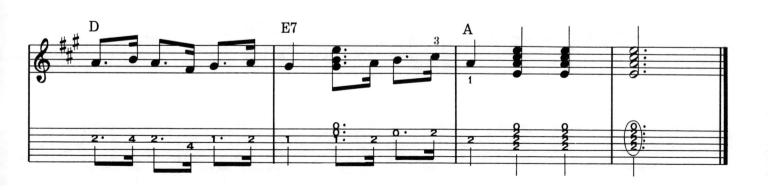

Mellowtone Waltz II

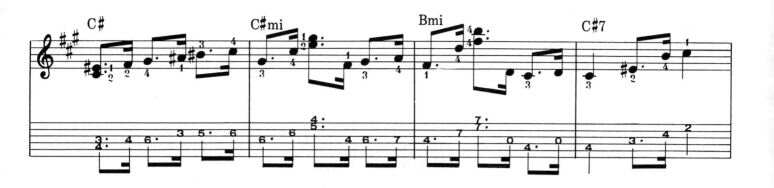

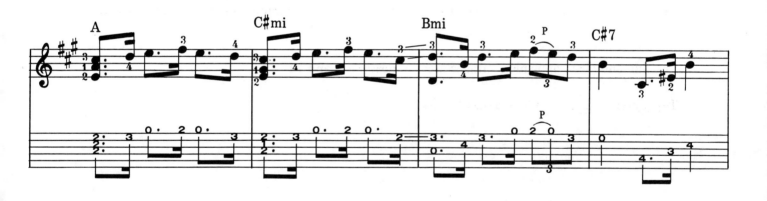
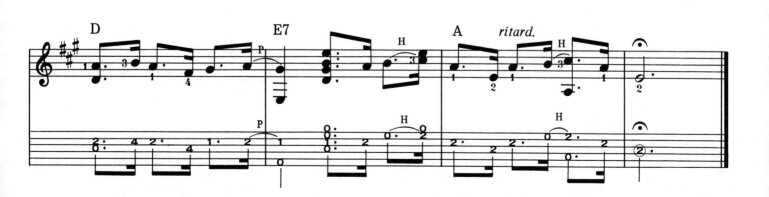

Morning Star

A simple tune in the key of C with a shuffle rhythm (♩ ♩. ♪). A tune like this reminds us that there can be beauty in simplicity.

Version One

. This arrangement is basically the melody with chord strums used as fillers.

. Be sure to pick the melody notes with an upstroke when they fall on an upbeat.

. Measure 12 requires an index finger half-barre across the first fret of the first three strings.

Version Two

. This version uses chord tones to harmonize under the melody (ex: measure 11), chords brushed between melody notes (ex: measure 1), single chord tones used as fillers (ex: the 1 and beat of measure one), arpeggios which follow melody notes (ex: measures 5 and 6) and hammered triplet fills (ex: measures 4, 7, 8). Be sure to use all these techniques in your own arranging.

. The slur and pick companion string is used in measures 2 and 14.

. The double-slide is used in measure 15.

Morning Star

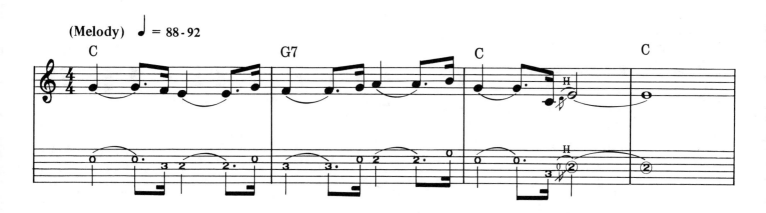

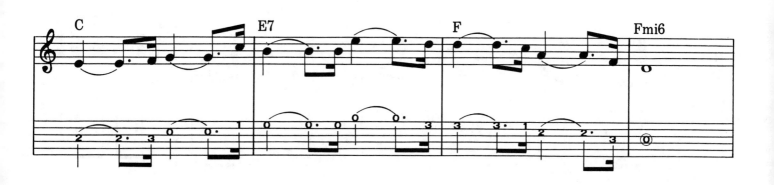

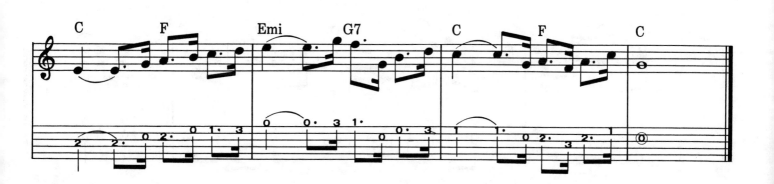

Morning Star I

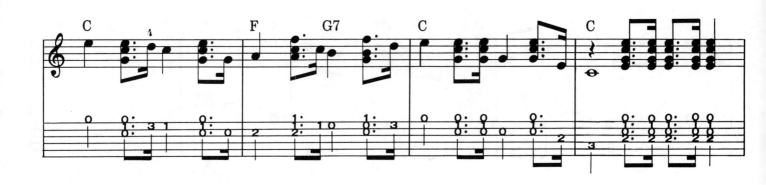

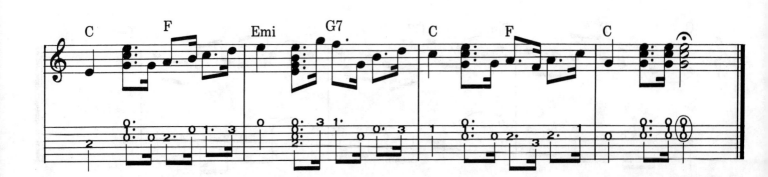

Morning Star II

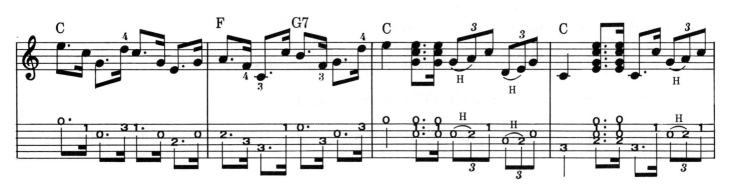

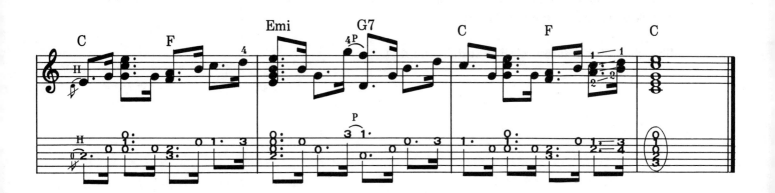

Orange Moon

Orange Moon is played with a shuffle feel in the key of A. The chord changes are standard and can be found in many tunes.

Version One

. The first finger plays all three fretted notes of the A chord in measure 1.

. Fourth position is used briefly in measures 1 and 9.

. Second position is used under the D♯ diminished chord in measures 3, 5, 11 and 13.

. Second position is also used under the F♯ 7 chord in measures 6 and 14.

. The slur and pick companion string technique is used in measure 15 going to 16 and at the end of measure 16.

Version Two

. Fifth position is used briefly in measures 1 and 9.

. The slur and pick companion string technique is used in measures 1, 9 and 14 - 15.

. The double stops on non-adjacent strings technique is used in measures 2, 8 and 10.

. A barre formation is used in measure 6.

. In measure 7 slide (∿∿) the C♯ note to the D♯ note, picking the D♯ with the middle finger while the pick plays the A note underneath it.

. Allow the notes in measure 16 to sustain and ring.

Orange Moon

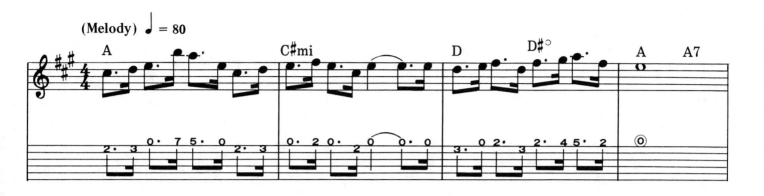

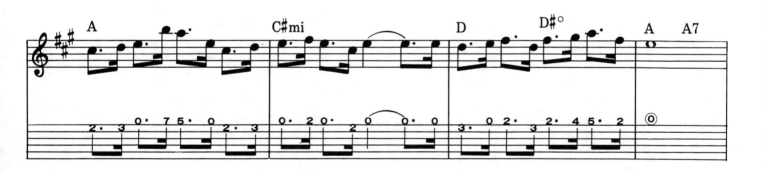

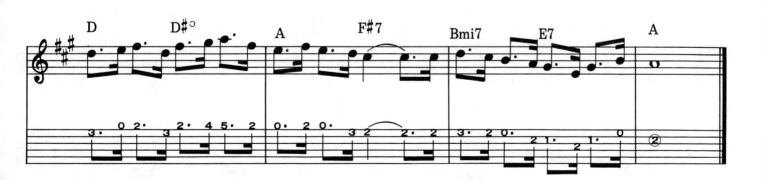

Orange Moon I

Orange Moon II

Spanish Moss

This Spanish - sounding waltz moves along quite rapidly. It has a mood quite unlike any other song in the book.

Version One

. This is really just the melody with a few chords thrown in as fillers.

. Some of the fingering is in second position and open strings are used where possible.

Version Two

. This is a stepped - up version of the melody with more closed fingerings.

. Watch the fingerings closely and also the position shifts in measures 5 and 13.

. This is a very good exercise for both hands. If it is difficult to play up to tempo, slow it down and practice with a metronome until the desired speed is attained.

Spanish Moss

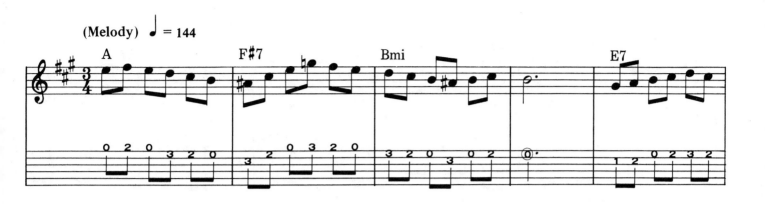

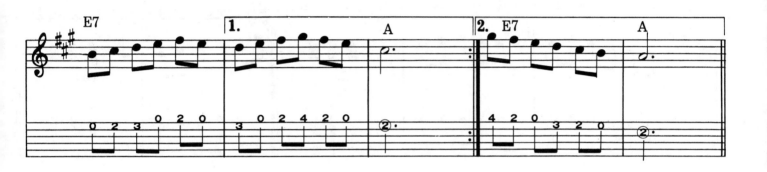

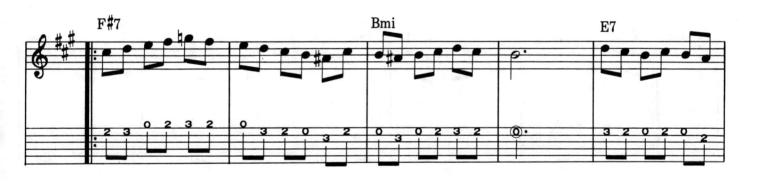

Spanish Moss I

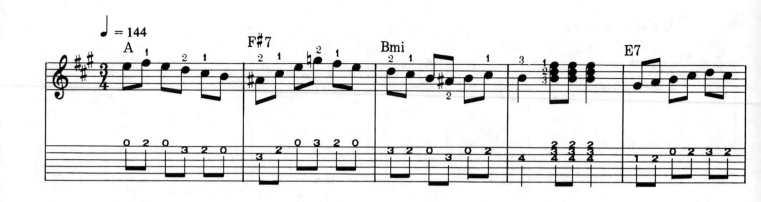

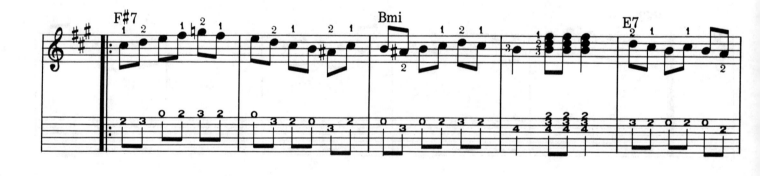

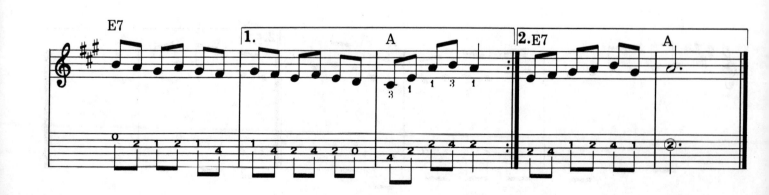

Spanish Moss II

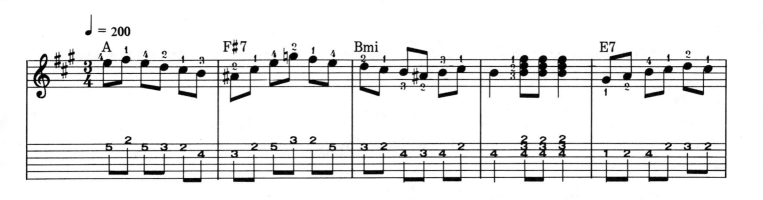

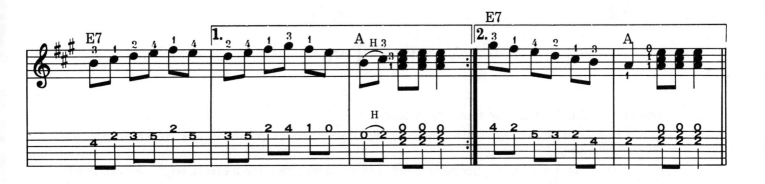

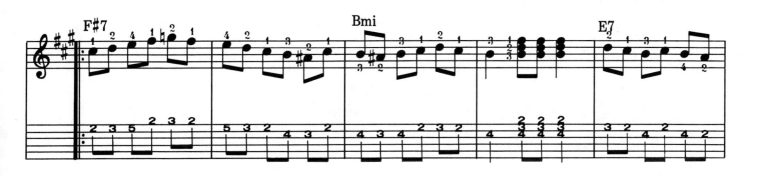

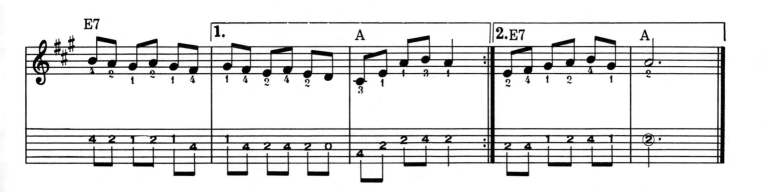

Strawberry Mountain

A fairly consistent rhythm (♩ ♫ ♫) that varies in the middle section. Basically slow and easy going, like a lazy day in the summer shade.

Version One

. This is a very simple adaptation of the melody.

. Do not rush the slides and hammers in this piece.

. If you wish, a slight ritard may be used at the end of measures 8, 12 and the end of the tune.

Version Two

. The melody should stand out above the arpeggios.

. The slur and and pick companion string technique is used quite regularly through this arrangement to fill out the sound.

. Double stops on non-adjacent strings are played twice in succession in measure ten. Note the position shift from one to the other.

. The grace note slides in measures 8 and 20 should be played smoothly yet rapidly.

. Notice the slide and subsequent fingerings in measure 11.

. The half-barre is used in measure 12.

Strawberry Mountain

Strawberry Mountain I

Strawberry Mountain II

MEL BAY PUBLICATIONS, INC. • PACIFIC, MISSOURI 63069

MEL BAY PUBLICATIONS, INC. • PACIFIC, MISSOURI 63069

MEL BAY PUBLICATIONS, INC. • PACIFIC, MISSOURI 63069

MEL BAY PUBLICATIONS, INC. • PACIFIC, MISSOURI 63069

MEL BAY PUBLICATIONS, INC. • PACIFIC, MISSOURI 63069

 MEL BAY PUBLICATIONS, INC. • PACIFIC, MISSOURI 63069

MEL BAY PUBLICATIONS, INC. • PACIFIC, MISSOURI 63069